Spelling, Punctuation & Grammar Made Easy

Key Stage 2
AGES 8–9

Author Claire White
Consultant Amy O'Connor

Certificate

Congratulations to

....

(write your name here)

for successfully finishing this book.

GOOD JOB!

You're a star.

AGES 8–9

Key Stage 2

Date

DK Penguin Random House

DK London
Editors Elizabeth Blakemore, Jolyon Goddard
Managing Editor Christine Stroyan
Managing Art Editor Anna Hall
Senior Production Editor Andy Hilliard
Senior Production Controller Jude Crozier
Jacket Design Development Manager Sophia MTT
Publisher Andrew Macintyre
Associate Publishing Director Liz Wheeler
Art Director Karen Self
Publishing Director Jonathan Metcalf

DK Delhi
Project Editor Neha Ruth Samuel
Senior Art Editor Stuti Tiwari Bhatia
Editor Nandini Gupta
Art Editor Rashika Kachroo
Assistant Art Editor Radhika Kapoor
Managing Editors Soma B. Chowdhury, Kingshuk Ghoshal
Managing Art Editors Ahlawat Gunjan, Govind Mittal
DTP Designers Anita Yadav, Rakesh Kumar, Harish Aggarwal
Senior Jacket Designer Suhita Dharamjit
Jackets Editorial Coordinator Priyanka Sharma

This edition published in 2020
First published in Great Britain in 2015 by Dorling Kindersley Limited
DK, One Embassy Gardens, 8 Viaduct Gardens, London, SW11 7BW

Copyright © 2015, 2020 Dorling Kindersley Limited
A Penguin Random House Company
10 9 8 7 6
006–270530–May/2020

A CIP catalogue record for this book is available from the British Library.
ISBN: 978-0-2411-8272-7

Printed and bound in Scotland

All images © Dorling Kindersley Limited
For further information see: www.dkimages.com

For the curious

www.dk.com

Contents

This chart lists all of the topics in the book. Once you have completed each page, colour in a star in the correct box below. When you have finished the book, sign and date the certificate.

★ Adjectives

There are three forms of adjectives: **positive**, **comparative** and **superlative**.

The positive is the simplest form. For example: a **strong** table. The comparative is used when comparing two people or things. For example: my book is **bigger** than yours (big). The superlative is used when three or more things are compared. For example: I ate the **largest** piece of cake (large).

Help Melissa the Monster write the comparative form of the adjectives.

Mia's dress ribbon is (long) _____ than her hair ribbon.

Marlon's roar was (loud) _____ than the other monster's roar.

Winter seems (dark) _____ than any other season.

The monster I just played with was (happy) _____ than the monster I played with yesterday.

I feel (good) _____ than I did when I woke up this morning.

My fur is (soft) _____ than my friend's fur.

Now help Melissa by writing the superlative form of the adjectives.

That is the (bad) _____ cake I have ever eaten!

Millie is the (quiet) _____ member of the family.

My dad is the (tall) _____ member of my monster family.

Mabel the Monster is the (busy) _____ monster I know.

Derek is the (large) _____ monster of them all.

A **prefix** is a group of letters that can be added to the beginning of a **root word** to change its meaning. For example: **un** + **happy** = **unhappy**.

In the box are some of the less common prefixes we use in the English language. Choose the correct prefix for each of the root words given below. You can use the same prefix more than once.

anti	super	auto

..............septic

..............hero

..............market

..............sonic

..............social

..............mobile

★ Suffixes

Suffixes are groups of letters, such as **ment**, **ness**, **ful** or **less**, added to the end of a root word to change its meaning. Suffixes are not complete words and cannot be used on their own in a sentence. For example: **care** + **ful** = **careful**.

Fill in the correct suffix to complete each of these word sums.

move + ... = movement

forgive + ... = forgiveness

power + ... = powerful

end + ... = endless

Now fill in the missing root word in each of these word sums.

.... + ment = payment

.... + ness = sickness

.... + ful = forceful

.... + less = fearless

Use the given root word and suffix to complete each of these word sums.

treat + ment = ...

sad + ness = ...

success + ful = ...

use + less = ...

The suffixes **sion** and **tion** both form nouns. They mean **state of** or **act of** and are pronounced (but never spelled) **shun**.
For example: **situate** + **tion** = **situation** and **confess** + **sion** = **confession**.

Underline the **shun** sound in each of the words below.
Then, write a sentence with each word.

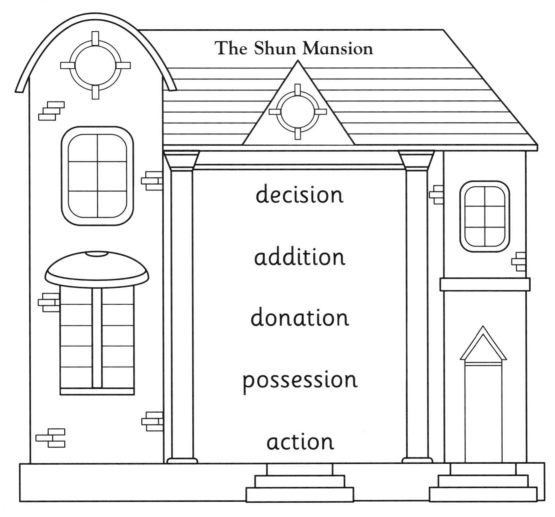

The Shun Mansion

decision

addition

donation

possession

action

....

....

....

....

....

Word families are groups of words that are closely related to each other.
Members of a word family may look similar or have related meanings.
For example: **harm** and **harmful**.

Look at the words in the box and then match them into family pairs.
The first one has been done for you.

familiar	appoint	disappoint	discussion
fly	discuss	flying	familiarity
correct	argue	incorrect	alive
peace	living	argument	peaceful

....familiar....   ....familiarity....

....

....

....

....

....

....

Bigger word families

Words that can be grouped into word families usually share a common **root word**. For example: **builder** and **building** share the root word **build**.

Some word families are much bigger. Place the words in the box below into their families in the same way you did on the opposite page.

approachable	exporter	estimate	approaching
exporting	estimating	approached	exports
estimation	approaches	exported	estimated

....　..........................　..........................　..........................

....　..........................　..........................　..........................

....　..........................　..........................　..........................

This last family also has four members. Make sentences using each of these words.

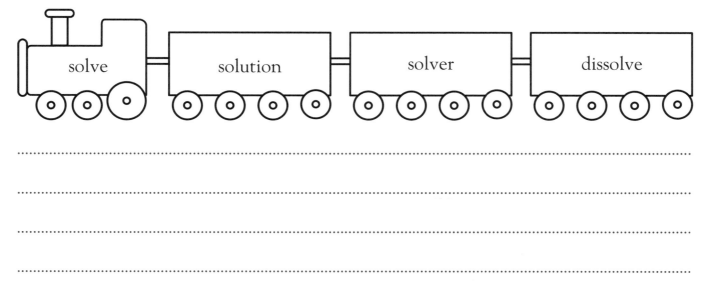

solve　solution　solver　dissolve

....

....

....

★ Pronouns

A **pronoun** is a word that can take the place of a noun. Pronouns that replace the subject of a sentence are called subject pronouns. They are **I, you** (singular and plural), **he, she, it, we** and **they**.
For example: **Matilda** ran fast. ⟶ **She** ran fast.

Draw lines between the words on the left and the correct pronoun on the right.

Danna and I   they

Joseph   it

Alice   he

the huge lorry   she

Katy and Eleanor   we

Write a pronoun that could replace the underlined word(s) in each sentence below.

<u>Zoe</u> loves to dance. ....

<u>Zoe and Issie</u> enjoy listening to Claire's singing. ....

<u>Claire</u> will sing a duet with Gail. ....

<u>Gail</u> has a beautiful voice, too. ....

<u>The concert</u> will be tomorrow evening. ....

<u>Issie and I</u> will be sitting in the front row. ....

<u>Oscar</u> will clap the loudest. ....

A **concrete noun** is the name of something we recognise with our senses. We can see, hear, feel, touch, taste or smell it, such as a **bicycle**, **song** or **slice of toast**. An **abstract noun**, on the other hand, names a concept or feeling, such as **imagination** or **sadness**, which our senses cannot recognise.

Can you help Leon fish out the abstract nouns? Draw lines from the rod to the fish with the abstract nouns on them.

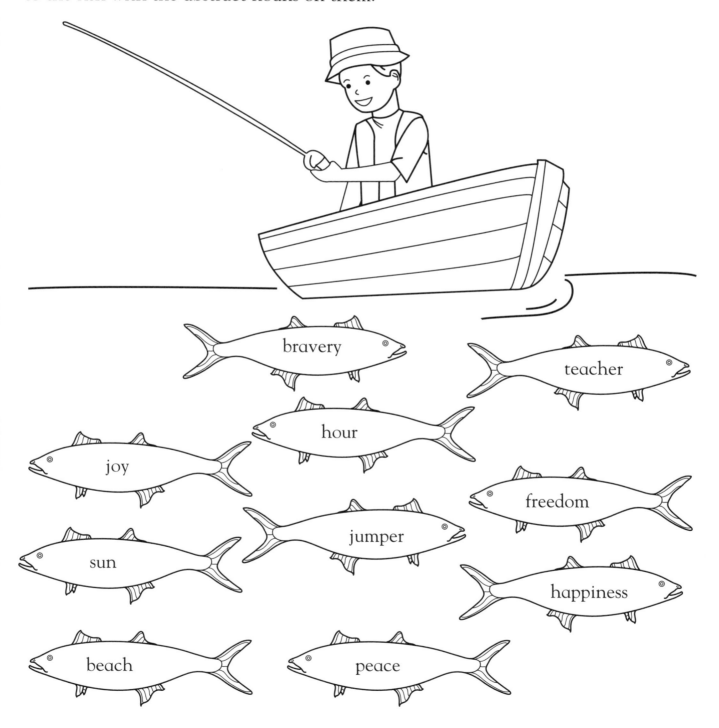

★ Saying it right!

FACTS

Reading sentences aloud can help you spot mistakes in your grammar.

Troy and Joy are aliens from another planet and they are learning to speak English. Help them by making corrections to their spoken language. Circle the incorrect words and then rewrite their sentences by using the correct words.

I maked a cake yesterday.

I thinked about what I needed to do.

My mum waked me up this morning.

I was so fast when I runned home.

Textspeak is used for writing text messages. It uses numbers and short forms of words instead of the usual sentence structure and lets you write messages quickly. **Remember**: avoid using textspeak in school work or formal written English.

Look at the text messages on each mobile phone. Troy the Alien does not understand textspeak. Help him by translating the text messages. Write the translations under each phone.

r u cmng tmrw?

....

Good to c u 2day.

B4 u r 2 tired please call me.

....

I luv u 4ever.

Evry1 startd sayin I shd txt him.

....

FACTS

A title can be a name of a book, a movie or a play, such as *The Lion King* and *Harry Potter and the Goblet of Fire*. You should always use capital, or upper-case, letters for the first, last and major words in titles.

Draw a line under the letters that should be capital in each book's title.

the lion,
the witch
and the wardrobe

the very hungry
caterpillar

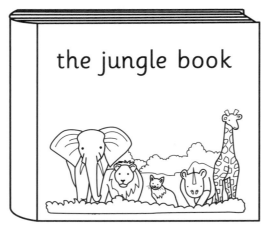

the jungle book

train your brain
to be a genius

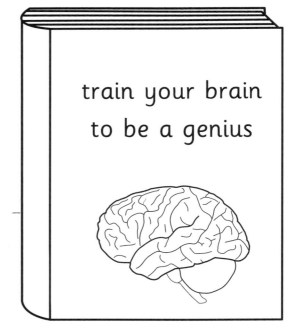

Think of two more book titles you know and write them with the correct capital letters.

....

....

FACTS

Verbs are doing words. A verb can express a physical action (as in **I walk**), a mental action (as in **he thinks**) or a state of being (as in **they live**). With **regular verbs**, the past tense ends in **ed**, as in **I loved** or **he baked**. Verbs that don't follow this rule are called **irregular verbs**, as in **he struck** or **we sang**.

The following irregular verbs are written in the past tense.
Write the present tense for each.

Past tense	Present tense
I felt	....
he put	....
they chose	....
we gave	....
Jane swam	....
you left	....
Thomas and I caught	....

Write two versions of a sentence for each verb pair below. **Remember**: use the present tense for the first sentence and the past tense for the second sentence.

rise ....

rose ....

sweep ....

swept ....

sit ....

sat ....

bring ....

brought ....

It can be confusing to decide whether to use **a** or **an**. The sound of a word's first letter determines which to use. If the word starts with a vowel sound, you should use **an**, as in **an hour** or **an umbrella**. If it starts with a consonant sound, you should use **a**, as in **a kettle** or **a year**.

Zoe needs your help! She is not sure if the sentences she has written use **a** and **an** correctly. Read these sentences and then put a tick (✓) if they are correct and a cross (✗) if they are incorrect. If the sentence is incorrect, write it correctly underneath to help Zoe.

I would like to have toast and a egg for my breakfast.

....

Last year I met a famous footballer.

....

I don't have time to find an extra jumper to wear.

....

I will buy you an present for your birthday.

....

I'm going to compete in a eight-kilometre run next month.

....

The key factor when thinking about the use of **a** or **an** before a word is the **sound**. It is not always a question of whether the word starts with a **vowel**. It is a question of whether it starts with a **vowel sound**.

For each of these sentences, circle **a** or **an** depending on which one you think is correct. Be sure to read the sentences aloud as this will help you make your choice. The correct answer will sound right.

It would be an / a honour to rescue you.

A magical pixie was hunting for an / a unicorn.

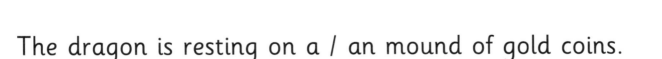

An angry elf took an / a hour to mix the potion.

The fairy broke her arm and would need an / a X-ray.

The dwarf is baking an / a apple pie.

The pixie flew down a / an one-way street.

The dragon is resting on a / an mound of gold coins.

Write a sentence using **a** and then another using **an**.

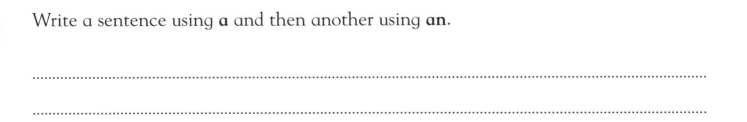

....

....

A **connective** is a word that is used to join sentences, phrases or words. **Connectives** are also known as conjunctions. Examples include **and**, **but** and **so**.

Each sentence below is missing a connective. Using the words from the box, rewrite each sentence with the correct connective in the correct place.

and	but	or	so	because	unless

We won't go to the park today it stops raining.

....

Alena is good at reading she has read many books from the library.

....

I like broccoli, I prefer carrots with my roast dinner.

....

Chris forgot to do his homework, he got into trouble with his mum.

....

You need to tidy your room you won't be allowed to have a friend around later.

....

Katy decided to go to bed she was tired.

....

Now write two sentences of your own using any two of the connectives from above.

....

....

Punctuation marks make writing easier to understand. They also help you add expression and intonation when reading aloud.

Are you up to a punctuation challenge? Draw lines to match each of the five types of punctuation mark first to its name and then to its definition.

| . | | comma | | This mark can be used to separate items in a list. It also shows where you can pause for a short time when you are reading. |

| ? | | full stop | | This mark is used to show where letters are missing in contractions, such as **don't**. It is also used to show who owns something, as in **Zoe's pen**. |

| , | | question mark | | These marks are used to show that someone is speaking. They are also called speech marks. |

| " " | | apostrophe | | This mark can be used at the end of a sentence. It shows where you can stop for breath when you are reading. |

| , | | inverted commas | | This mark is used when a question is being asked. It shows that you need to raise the tone of your voice when reading. |

Apostrophes can be used to show possession, or ownership. Before placing an apostrophe, the first thing you need to think about is whether the possessor is singular or plural. This is important because it tells you where you must put the apostrophe. For example: in **the dog's dinner**, the apostrophe goes before the **s** to show that the dinner belongs to just one (singular) dog. Whereas, in **the dogs' dinner**, the apostrophe goes after the **s** to show that the dinner belongs to more than one (plural) dog.

Marlon the Monster is in a bit of a muddle about apostrophes. Help him by marking whether the apostrophes to show possession are in the correct place in the sentences he has written. Put a tick (✔) next to the apostrophes used correctly and a cross (✗) next to those used incorrectly. Then write the correct sentences on the dotted lines.

It was the girl's dress I wanted to wear.

....

I found one womans' hat in the park.

....

There was a child's hat on the floor.

....

My room's door is jammed.

....

I saw the mans' coat hung on the back of the door.

....

The White's family home is near to where I landed my spacecraft.

....

FACTS

Using a **comma** in the correct place helps make a sentence's meaning clear. The incorrect placing of a comma can change the meaning of the sentence.

Read these sentences carefully. Then, match each sentence to the correct picture.

"Let's eat Helen," said Vanessa.

"Let's eat, Helen," said Vanessa.

Mrs White takes pleasure in cooking her friends and her cat.

Mrs White takes pleasure in cooking, her friends and her cat.

The commas are in the wrong places in this sentence. Rewrite the sentence with the commas in the correct places.

Arron Nicola and, Oscar went to the fancy-dress party as, Shrek Snow, White and a Smurf.

....

....

FACTS

The words spoken by a person in a piece of writing, such as a story, are called direct speech. We use **inverted commas**, or speech marks, to enclose direct speech. These quoted words are usually preceded or followed by an indication of who said them and how he or she said them. For example: **Tom shouted, "Watch out!"** or **"What's for dinner?" she asked**.

Rewrite the sentences in the bubbles on the dotted lines, adding inverted commas and who said them. You can use the words in the box below to help you describe how the words are said. The first one has been done for you.

begged	whispered	answered	snapped	muttered

I hope I will find a handsome prince.

I really am a handsome prince.

"I hope I will find a handsome prince," the princess whispered.

Hubble, bubble, mixing trouble.

Please be my friend.

At the end of a piece of speech, there should be a full stop, comma, exclamation mark or question mark. This punctuation mark is placed inside the closing inverted commas. Whenever a new speaker says something, start his or her speech on a new line. For example:

"Can I play outside now?" asked Rosie.
"Only after you've finished your homework," replied her mum.

Below is a cartoon strip of a conversation between the aliens Bee-Bee and Bo-Bo. Rewrite their speech as sentences, using the correct punctuation and starting a new line for each new speaker. Use some of the words in the box on the opposite page, or some of your own, to show how the sentences are said.

....

....

....

....

....

....

The words **there**, **their** and **they're** are homophones. These are words that sound the same but have different spellings and meanings.

Leon is fishing again, but this time he has some friends with him. Help them find the correct homophone to complete their sentences. Catch the correct word by drawing a line from each speech bubble to the fish with the right word on it.

Two words that often get mixed up are **off** and **of**.
The word **of** is a **preposition**, which connects nouns or pronouns to other words in a sentence. For example: the girl was the daughter **of** a police officer.
The word **off** is an **adverb**, which adds to the meaning of another word, usually a verb or an adjective. For example: did Madeleine jump **off** the swing?

Complete the sentences below by using either **of** or **off**.

It was time to turn .... the lantern.

The dragon jumped .... his nest to see who was coming.

The princess .... Wizardland took .... her shoes.

The Grand Goblin was in charge .... all goblins across the land.

The fairy was the most beautiful .... them all.

The pixie hung .... the branch .... the tree.

Now, write a sentence using **of** and another using **off**.

....

....

★ "Too" or "to"?

Two words that often get mixed up are the homophones **too** and **to**.
The word **too** means **as well**, as in **Leon came too**.
It is also used to give the idea of in excess, as in **that's too much**.
The word **to** is used as a preposition, as in **pass it to him**.
It can also be used to show the infinitive, or simplest form, of a verb,
as in **I want to play**.

Look at the sentences below. Circle the correct **to/too** in each sentence.

I can do it to / too.

I am going to / too the park.

Did you think that to / too?

The shoes were to / too expensive.

I want to / too run around the planet.

Did you tell her what to / too do first?

This cat is to / too chubby.

She handed the parcel to / too the postal worker.

Now see if you can write two sentences, one using **to** and the other using **too**.

....

....

FACTS

There are certain rules we can follow when making **plurals** of nouns (see the **Rule** column in the chart below).

However, there are some exceptions to the rules:

Certain nouns change a vowel sound when they become plural.

For example: **tooth/teeth**, **woman/women** and **mouse/mice**.

Some nouns don't change at all when they become plural.

For example: **deer**, **sheep** and **species**.

Choose words from the box below and write each one in the correct place on the chart. Then, write the singular or plural form of the word in the right place, too.

coat	books	buzz	churches	fox	countries
days	key	baby	plays	piano	
loaf		knives		videos	

Rule	Singular	Plural
For most nouns ending in **o**, add **s**.	radio	radios
For most nouns ending in **ch**, **sh**, **s**, **x** or **z**, add **es**.	hiss	hisses
For most nouns ending in a vowel and **y**, add **s**.	boy	boys
For most nouns ending in a consonant and **y**, drop the **y** and add **ies**.	lily	lilies
For most nouns ending in a single **f** or **fe**, change the **f** or **fe** to a **v** and add **es**.	half	halves
For most other nouns, just add **s**.	dog	dogs

★ Similes

FACTS

Similes are phrases that compare one thing to another, using the words **like** (for example: Liam roared **like** a lion) or **as** (for example: my grandad is **as** daft **as** a brush). Poems are a good, fun way of introducing similes.

Look in the word box to find the missing words in this simile poem. Write them in the spaces below.

| giraffe | welly | busy bee | billy goat | donkey | monkey |

Silly Similes

Here are some silly similes

To make you go, "Tee-hee!"

You're as silly as a .... ,

As manky as a .... ,

Smelly like an old .... ,

Wonky like a three-legged .... ,

And as crazy as a lazy ....

So... if you didn't have a laugh,

Then I'm about as funny as a .... !

Now read the completed poem aloud.

Expanding simple sentences by adding more information helps create a better picture in the readers' minds. It also makes writing more engaging.

Look at the pictures below and write sentences that describe them.
Use words from the box to make the sentences interesting.

| curly | magic | red | maths | bold | thunder |
| pointy | stripes | excitement | enchanted | strict | grumpy |

The teacher

....

....

....

The umbrella

....

....

....

The pixie

....

....

....

The woodland

....

....

....

A piece of writing, such as a story, is made up of paragraphs. Each paragraph usually deals with a single theme and is indicated by a new line with indentation, a small gap between the previous paragraph or, sometimes, numbering. Paragraphs can range from a single sentence to several sentences.

Whatever type of story you are writing, paragraphs help you structure it. When you plan a story, plan your paragraphs at the same time. Doing this helps you plot out the stages of the story, such as the opening, buildup, problem, resolution and ending. You can use a story mountain plan to help you.

Problem: she uses the pixie's magic to get herself everything she wants but becomes very selfish.

Resolution: Claire soon loses all her friends. She then uses the magic to make other people happy. After that, she returns the pixie to where she found it.

Buildup: she takes it home and secretly keeps it in her bedroom.

Ending: however, the next day someone else finds the pixie...

Opening: Claire discovers a magic pixie on her way home from school.

Think about each paragraph on the opposite page and use your imagination to answer the questions below.

Opening: what does the pixie look like?
Buildup: where does Claire keep it in her bedroom?
Problem: what does she ask the pixie to get for her?
Resolution: how does Claire feel when she helps her friends?
Ending: who will find the pixie next?

Now, write in your ideas in the boxes around the story mountain below. These don't have to be sentences. They can be key words that will remind you of your thoughts if you go on to write the full story.

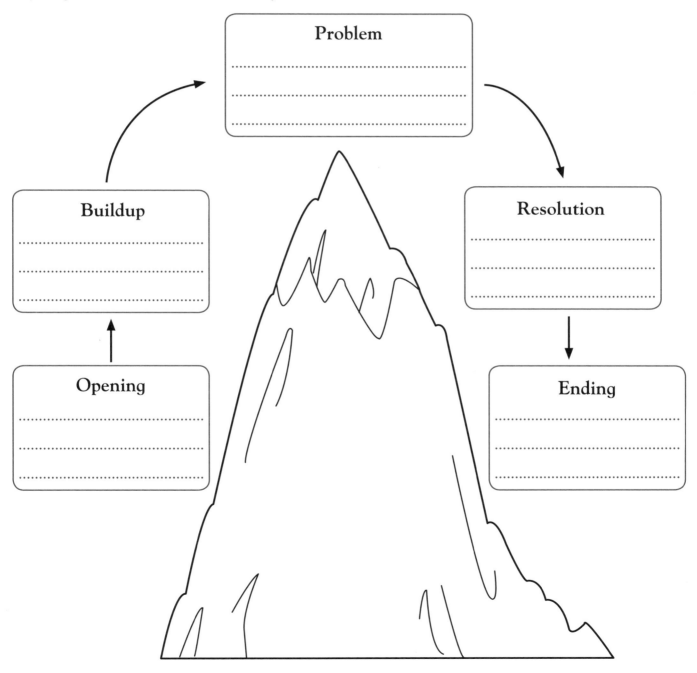

FACTS

Once you have learned the rules associated with spelling, including the use of prefixes and suffixes, it is easier to spell a wider range of words correctly. Another way to learn spelling is the look-cover-write-check method.

Follow the look-cover-write-check method, as shown below, to learn the spelling of the words listed on this page. If you are unsure of the meaning of any of these words, ask your parent to help you look them up in a dictionary.

1. Look (at the word)   **2.** Cover (the word)

3. Write (the word)    **4.** Check (to see if you got it right!)

medicine	....	address	....
believe	....	naughty	....
woman	....	various	....
through	....	knowledge	....
experience	....	quarter	....
reign	....	favourite	....
weight	....	separate	....
height	....	disappear	....
possess	....	occasion	....
island	....	grammar	....
library	....	centre	....

Answer section with parents' notes

Key Stage 2
Ages 8–9

This eight-page section provides answers and explanatory notes to all of the activities in this book, enabling you to assess your child's work.

Work through each page together and ensure that your child understands each task. Point out any mistakes your child makes and correct any spelling errors. (Your child should use the handwriting style taught at his or her school.) In addition to making corrections, it is very important to praise your child's efforts and achievements.

At the end of this section, there is a glossary that includes all of the key terms covered in this book.

★ Adjectives

FACTS There are three forms of adjectives: **positive**, **comparative** and **superlative**.

The positive is the simplest form. For example: a **strong** table. The comparative is used when comparing two people or things. For example: my book is **bigger** than yours (big). The superlative is used when three or more things are compared. For example: I ate the **largest** piece of cake (large).

Help Melissa the Monster write the comparative form of the adjectives.

Mia's dress ribbon is (long) __longer__ than her hair ribbon.

Marlon's roar was (loud) __louder__ than the other monster's roar.

Winter seems (dark) __darker__ than any other season.

The monster I just played with was (happy) __happier__ than the monster I played with yesterday.

I feel (good) __better__ than I did when I woke up this morning.

My fur is (soft) __softer__ than my friend's fur.

Now help Melissa by writing the superlative form of the adjectives.

That is the (bad) __worst__ cake I have ever eaten!

Millie is the (quiet) __quietest__ member of the family.

My dad is the (tall) __tallest__ member of my monster family.

Mabel the Monster is the (busy) __busiest__ monster I know.

Derek is the (large) __largest__ monster of them all.

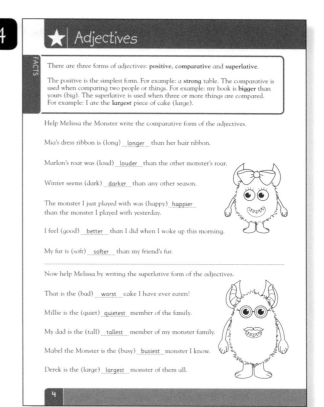

Encourage your child to identify other adjectives when reading. You may also like to encourage him or her to use adjectives to add details during a conversation.

Using prefixes ★

FACTS A **prefix** is a group of letters that can be added to the beginning of a **root word** to change its meaning. For example: **un** + **happy** = **unhappy**.

In the box are some of the less common prefixes we use in the English language. Choose the correct prefix for each of the root words given below. You can use the same prefix more than once.

anti	super	auto

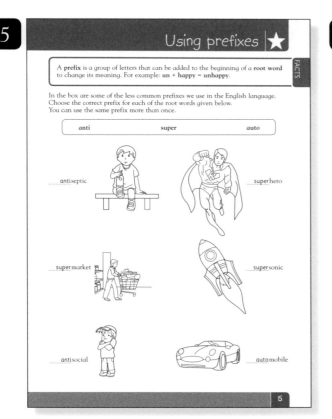

antiseptic

superhero

supermarket

supersonic

antisocial

automobile

Help your child think of other words with the prefixes discussed here. Look for **anti**, **super** and **auto** words in books that you read together. Encourage your child to tell you what the words mean and to identify each root word.

★ Suffixes

FACTS **Suffixes** are groups of letters, such as **ment**, **ness**, **ful** or **less**, added to the end of a root word to change its meaning. Suffixes are not complete words and cannot be used on their own in a sentence. For example: **care** + **ful** = **careful**.

Fill in the correct suffix to complete each of these word sums.

move + __ment__ = movement

forgive + __ness__ = forgiveness

power + __ful__ = powerful

end + __less__ = endless

Now fill in the missing root word in each of these word sums.

__pay__ + ment = payment

__sick__ + ness = sickness

__force__ + ful = forceful

__fear__ + less = fearless

Use the given root word and suffix to complete each of these word sums.

treat + ment = __treatment__

sad + ness = __sadness__

success + ful = __successful__

use + less = __useless__

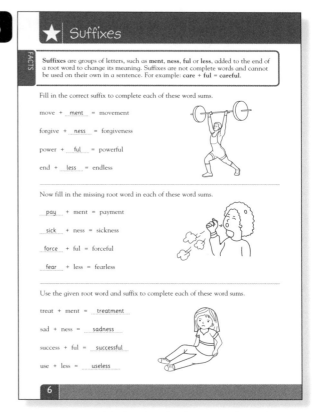

Help your child think of other words with the suffixes on this page. Look for **ment**, **less**, **ful** and **ness** words in books that you read together. Ask your child to tell you what each word means.

The suffixes "sion" and "tion" ★

FACTS

The suffixes **sion** and **tion** both form nouns. They mean **state of** or **act of** and are pronounced (but never spelled) **shun**.
For example: **situate + tion = situation** and **confess + sion = confession**.

Underline the **shun** sound in each of the words below.
Then, write a sentence with each word.

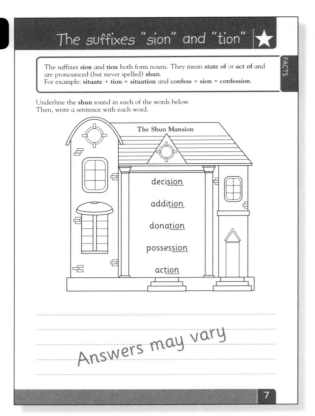

The Shun Mansion

deci<u>sion</u>

addi<u>tion</u>

dona<u>tion</u>

posse<u>ssion</u>

ac<u>tion</u>

Answers may vary

7

Whenever your child writes words ending in **tion** or **sion**, remind him or her that the suffix is never spelled **shun**. Ask your child to recall the spelling options to help him or her select the correct one.

★ Word families

FACTS

Word families are groups of words that are closely related to each other. Members of a word family may look similar or have related meanings.
For example: **harm** and **harmful**.

Look at the words in the box and then match them into family pairs.
The first one has been done for you.

familiar	appoint	disappoint	discussion
fly	discuss	flying	familiarity
correct	argue	incorrect	alive
peace	living	argument	peaceful

familiar   familiarity

alive   living

discuss   discussion

argue   argument

fly   flying

correct   incorrect

appoint   disappoint

peace   peaceful

8

See if you and your child can make a list of other word families.

Bigger word families ★

FACTS

Words that can be grouped into word families usually share a common **root word**. For example: **builder** and **building** share the root word **build**.

Some word families are much bigger. Place the words in the box below into their families in the same way you did on the opposite page.

approachable	exporter	estimate	approaching
exporting	estimating	approached	exports
estimation	approaches	exported	estimated

estimate   estimated   estimation   estimating

approachable   approached   approaches   approaching

exported   exporter   exporting   exports

This last family also has four members. Make sentences using each of these words.

solve   solution   solver   dissolve

Answers may vary

9

When reading with your child, ask if he or she can find words from the word families you have explored in this book. Talk to your child about the spelling similarities in these words.

★ Pronouns

FACTS

A **pronoun** is a word that can take the place of a noun. Pronouns that replace the subject of a sentence are called subject pronouns. They are **I, you** (singular and plural), **he, she, it, we** and **they**.
For example: **Matilda** ran fast. → **She** ran fast.

Draw lines between the words on the left and the correct pronoun on the right.

Danna and I   they

Joseph   it

Alice   he

the huge lorry   she

Katy and Eleanor   we

Write a pronoun that could replace the underlined word(s) in each sentence below.

<u>Zoe</u> loves to dance.   She

<u>Zoe and Issie</u> enjoy listening to Claire's singing.   They

<u>Claire</u> will sing a duet with Gail.   She

<u>Gail</u> has a beautiful voice, too.   She

<u>The concert</u> will be tomorrow evening.   It

<u>Issie and I</u> will be sitting in the front row.   We

<u>Oscar</u> will clap the loudest.   He

10

Ask your child to say aloud some sentences that use a pronoun instead of a proper name. Ask him or her to identify the pronouns used.

Abstract nouns ★

FACTS

A **concrete noun** is the name of something we recognise with our senses. We can see, hear, feel, touch, taste or smell it, such as a **bicycle**, **song** or **slice of toast**. An **abstract noun**, on the other hand, names a concept or feeling, such as **imagination** or **sadness**, which our senses cannot recognise.

Can you help Leon fish out the abstract nouns? Draw lines from the rod to the fish with the abstract nouns on them.

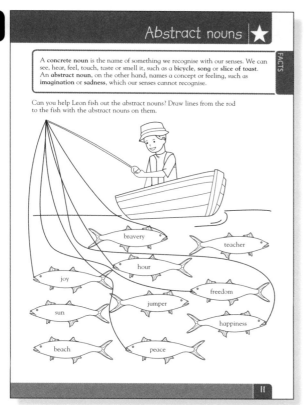

Ask your child to explain why the nouns that were not selected in the exercise are not abstract nouns.

★ Saying it right!

FACTS

Reading sentences aloud can help you spot mistakes in your grammar.

Troy and Joy are aliens from another planet and they are learning to speak English. Help them by making corrections to their spoken language. Circle the incorrect words and then rewrite their sentences by using the correct words.

It is important to correct your child's spoken grammatical mistakes. If your child says, for example, "I maked a cake" correct him or her by saying, "You **made** a cake, not **maked** a cake."

Textspeak ★

FACTS

Textspeak is used for writing text messages. It uses numbers and short forms of words instead of the usual sentence structure and lets you write messages quickly. **Remember**: avoid using textspeak in school work or formal written English.

Look at the text messages on each mobile phone. Troy the Alien does not understand textspeak. Help him by translating the text messages. Write the translations under each phone.

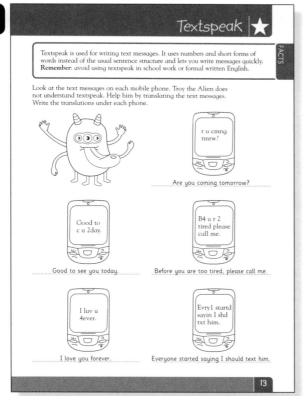

Talk to your child about how important it is to refrain from using textspeak in his or her written work. Encourage him or her to spot this type of writing in everyday life. It can often be seen on adverts or posters.

★ Capital letters in titles

FACTS

A title can be a name of a book, a movie or a play, such as *The Lion King* and *Harry Potter and the Goblet of Fire*. You should always use capital, or upper-case, letters for the first, last and major words in titles.

Draw a line under the letters that should be capital in each book's title.

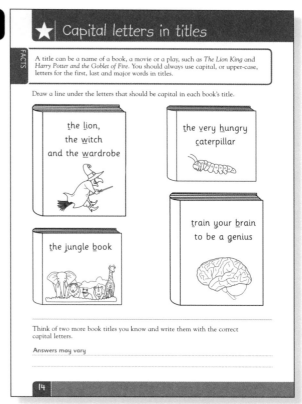

Think of two more book titles you know and write them with the correct capital letters.

Answers may vary

Point out examples of capital letters in books you read together and signs you see. Also encourage your child to spot errors in the use of capital letters.

Irregular verbs ★

FACTS

Verbs are doing words. A verb can express a physical action (as in **I walk**), a mental action (as in **he thinks**) or a state of being (as in **they live**). With **regular verbs**, the past tense ends in **ed**, as in **I loved** or **he baked**. Verbs that don't follow this rule are called **irregular verbs**, as in **he struck** or **we sang**.

The following irregular verbs are written in the past tense. Write the present tense for each.

Past tense	Present tense
I felt	I feel
he put	he puts
they chose	they choose
we gave	we give
Jane swam	Jane swims
you left	you leave
Thomas and I caught	Thomas and I catch

Write two versions of a sentence for each verb pair below. **Remember**: use the present tense for the first sentence and the past tense for the second sentence.

rise
rose

sweep
swept

Answers may vary

sit
sat

bring
brought

Encourage your child to find more examples of irregular verbs in books and magazines or online.

★ Using "a" or "an"

FACTS

It can be confusing to decide whether to use **a** or **an**. The sound of a word's first letter determines which to use. If the word starts with a vowel sound, you should use **an**, as in **an hour** or **an umbrella**. If it starts with a consonant sound, you should use **a**, as in **a kettle** or **a year**.

Zoe needs your help! She is not sure if the sentences she has written use **a** and **an** correctly. Read these sentences and then put a tick (✓) if they are correct and a cross (✗) if they are incorrect. If the sentence is incorrect, write it correctly underneath to help Zoe.

I would like to have toast and a egg for my breakfast.

I would like to have toast and an egg for my breakfast. ✗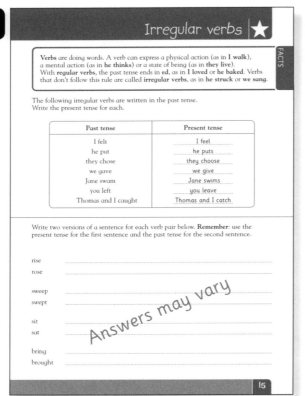

Last year I met a famous footballer. ✓

I don't have time to find an extra jumper to wear. ✓

I will buy you an present for your birthday.

I will buy you a present for your birthday. ✗

I'm going to compete in a eight-kilometre run next month.

I'm going to compete in an eight-kilometre run next month. ✗

Encourage your child to spot the use of **a** and **an** when you read together. Remind him or her when **an** should be used.

More "a" or "an" ★

FACTS

The key factor when thinking about the use of **a** or **an** before a word is the **sound**. It is not always a question of whether the word starts with a **vowel**. It is a question of whether it starts with a **vowel sound**.

For each of these sentences, circle **a** or **an** depending on which one you think is correct. Be sure to read the sentences aloud as this will help you make your choice. The correct answer will sound right.

It would be (an)/ a honour to rescue you.

A magical pixie was hunting for an /(a)unicorn.

An angry elf took (an)/ a hour to mix the potion.

The fairy broke her arm and would need (an)/ a X-ray.

The dwarf is baking (an)/ a apple pie.

The pixie flew down(a)/ an one-way street.

The dragon is resting on(a)/ an mound of gold coins.

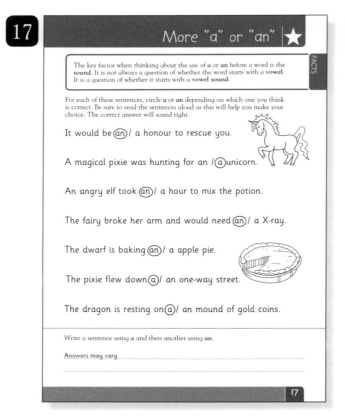

Write a sentence using **a** and then another using **an**.

Answers may vary

Point out to your child when he or she naturally uses **an** in his or her spoken language because it sounds right.

★ Connectives

FACTS

A **connective** is a word that is used to join sentences, phrases or words. **Connectives** are also known as conjunctions. Examples include **and**, **but** and **so**.

Each sentence below is missing a connective. Using the words from the box, rewrite each sentence with the correct connective in the correct place.

and	but	or	so	because	unless

We won't go to the park today it stops raining.
We won't go to the park today unless it stops raining.

Alena is good at reading she has read many books from the library.
Alena is good at reading and she has read many books from the library.

I like broccoli, I prefer carrots with my roast dinner.
I like broccoli, but I prefer carrots with my roast dinner.

Chris forgot to do his homework, he got into trouble with his mum.
Chris forgot to do his homework, so he got into trouble with his mum.

You need to tidy your room you won't be allowed to have a friend around later.
You need to tidy your room or you won't be allowed to have a friend around later.

Katy decided to go to bed she was tired.
Katy decided to go to bed because she was tired.

Now write two sentences of your own using any two of the connectives from above.
Answers may vary

Check the sentences to ensure the connectives have been used correctly. When your child is writing his or her own sentences, encourage the use of connectives to extend the sentences.

Punctuation marks ★

FACTS

Punctuation marks make writing easier to understand. They also help you add expression and intonation when reading aloud.

Are you up to a punctuation challenge? Draw lines to match each of the five types of punctuation mark first to its name and then to its definition.

.		comma		This mark can be used to separate items in a list. It also shows where you can pause for a short time when you are reading.
?		full stop		This mark is used to show where letters are missing in contractions, such as **don't**. It is also used to show who owns something, as in **Zoe's pen**.
,		question mark		These marks are used to show that someone is speaking. They are also called speech marks.
" "		apostrophe		This mark can be used at the end of a sentence. It shows where you can stop for breath when you are reading.
,		inverted commas		This mark is used when a question is being asked. It shows that you need to raise the tone of your voice when reading.

Encourage your child to pay attention to punctuation marks when reading. In particular, remind him or her to take a short pause for a comma and a longer one for a full stop.

★ Apostrophe to show possession

FACTS

Apostrophes can be used to show possession, or ownership. Before placing an apostrophe, the first thing you need to think about is whether the possessor is singular or plural. This is important because it tells you where you must put the apostrophe. For example: in **the dog's dinner**, the apostrophe goes before the **s** to show that the dinner belongs to just one (singular) dog. Whereas, in **the dogs' dinner**, the apostrophe goes after the **s** to show that the dinner belongs to more than one (plural) dog.

Marlon the Monster is in a bit of a muddle about apostrophes. Help him by marking whether the apostrophes to show possession are in the correct place in the sentences he has written. Put a tick (✓) next to the apostrophes used correctly and a cross (✗) next to those used incorrectly. Then write the correct sentences on the dotted lines.

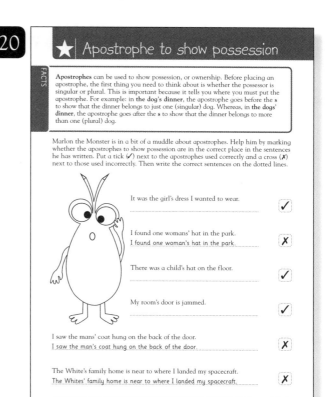

It was the girl's dress I wanted to wear. ✓

I found one womans' hat in the park.
I found one woman's hat in the park. ✗

There was a child's hat on the floor. ✓

My room's door is jammed. ✓

I saw the mans' coat hung on the back of the door.
I saw the man's coat hung on the back of the door. ✗

The White's family home is near to where I landed my spacecraft.
The Whites' family home is near to where I landed my spacecraft. ✗

Encourage your child to use an apostrophe to show possession in his or her own writing. You can also encourage your child to spot this kind of apostrophe usage when reading.

Comma sense ★

FACTS

Using a **comma** in the correct place helps make a sentence's meaning clear. The incorrect placing of a comma can change the meaning of the sentence.

Read these sentences carefully. Then, match each sentence to the correct picture.

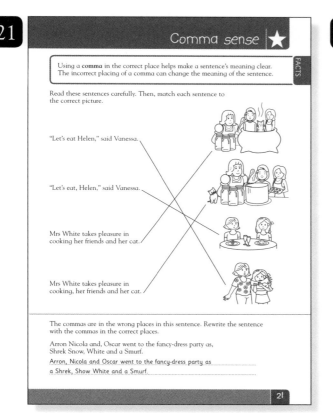

"Let's eat Helen," said Vanessa.

"Let's eat, Helen," said Vanessa.

Mrs White takes pleasure in cooking her friends and her cat.

Mrs White takes pleasure in cooking, her friends and her cat.

The commas are in the wrong places in this sentence. Rewrite the sentence with the commas in the correct places.

Arron Nicola and, Oscar went to the fancy-dress party as, Shrek Snow, White and a Smurf.
Arron, Nicola and Oscar went to the fancy-dress party as a Shrek, Show White and a Smurf.

Demonstrate to your child how each sentence sounds when the punctuation is correctly and incorrectly placed. Then, invite your child to try saying the sentences – with and without the commas – aloud.

★ Direct speech

FACTS

The words spoken by a person in a piece of writing, such as a story, are called direct speech. We use **inverted commas**, or speech marks, to enclose direct speech. These quoted words are usually preceded or followed by an indication of who said them and how he or she said them. For example: **Tom shouted, "Watch out!"** or **"What's for dinner?" she asked**.

Rewrite the sentences in the bubbles on the dotted lines, adding inverted commas and who said them. You can use the words in the box below to help you describe how the words are said. The first one has been done for you.

begged	whispered	answered	snapped	muttered

Answers may vary

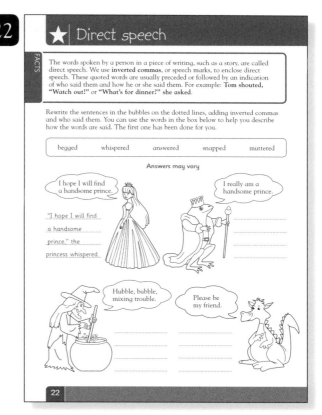

I hope I will find a handsome prince.

"I hope I will find a handsome prince," the princess whispered.

I really am a handsome prince.

Hubble, bubble, mixing trouble.

Please be my friend.

Encourage your child to look out for inverted commas when characters are speaking in books and magazines. Point out that it is only what the character actually says that appears within the inverted commas.

More direct speech ★

FACTS

At the end of a piece of speech, there should be a full stop, comma, exclamation mark or question mark. This punctuation mark is placed inside the closing inverted commas. Whenever a new speaker says something, start his or her speech on a new line. For example:
"Can I play outside now?" asked Rosie.
"Only after you've finished your homework," replied her mum.

Below is a cartoon strip of a conversation between the aliens Bee-Bee and Bo-Bo. Rewrite their speech as sentences, using the correct punctuation and starting a new line for each new speaker. Use some of the words in the box on the opposite page, or some of your own, to show how the sentences are said.

Bee-Bee, I don't understand all this business with inverted commas, do you!

Can you explain it to me then, please?

I'm sorry. I just feel very confused.

Bo-Bo, it's really very simple.

There's no need to get so cross!

Okay, let's begin!

Answers may vary

23

If you are reading with your child and the text says the character whispers, then read the speech in a whispering voice to demonstrate expression. Also, talk to your child about how the punctuation at the end of a sentence might change how you read something out.

★ "There", "their" or "they're"?

FACTS

The words **there**, **their** and **they're** are homophones. These are words that sound the same but have different spellings and meanings.

Leon is fishing again, but this time he has some friends with him. Help them find the correct homophone to complete their sentences. Catch the correct word by drawing a line from each speech bubble to the fish with the right word on it.

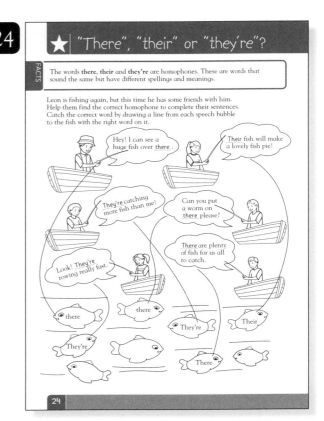

Hey! I can see a huge fish over there .

Their fish will make a lovely fish pie!

They're catching more fish than me!

Can you put a worm on there please?

There are plenty of fish for us all to catch.

Look! They're rowing really fast.

there | there | They're | Their

They're | They're | There

24

When your child is writing, remind him or her which of these homophones he or she should use. Encourage him or her to spot them when reading and to look at the context in which these words have been used.

"Off" or "of"? ★

FACTS

Two words that often get mixed up are **off** and **of**.
The word **of** is a preposition, which connects nouns or pronouns to other words in a sentence. For example: the girl was the daughter **of** a police officer.
The word **off** is an adverb, which adds to the meaning of another word, usually a verb or an adjective. For example: did Madeleine jump **off** the swing?

Complete the sentences below by using either **of** or **off**.

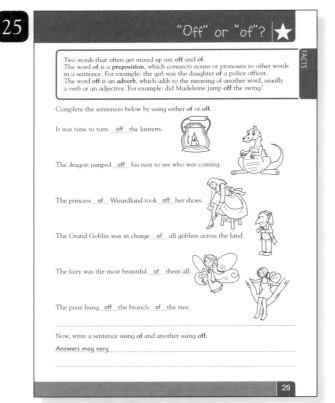

It was time to turn __off__ the lantern.

The dragon jumped __off__ his nest to see who was coming.

The princess __of__ Wizardland took __off__ her shoes.

The Grand Goblin was in charge __of__ all goblins across the land.

The fairy was the most beautiful __of__ them all.

The pixie hung __off__ the branch __of__ the tree.

Now, write a sentence using **of** and another using **off**.

Answers may vary

25

When your child writes sentences using these words, ensure you check his or her spelling. Praise your child when he or she has remembered to use the correct word.

★ "Too" or "to"?

FACTS

Two words that often get mixed up are the homophones **too** and **to**.
The word **too** means **as well**, as in **Leon came too**.
It is also used to give the idea of in excess, as in **that's too much**.
The word **to** is used as a preposition, as in **pass it to him**.
It can also be used to show the infinitive, or simplest form, of a verb, as in **I want to play**.

Look at the sentences below. Circle the correct **to/too** in each sentence.

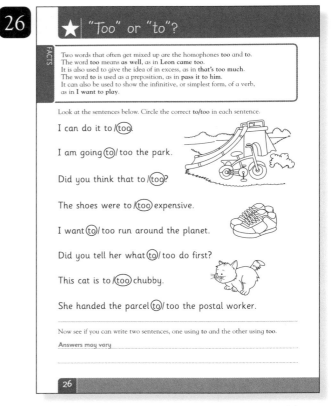

I can do it to /(too).

I am going (to)/ too the park.

Did you think that to /(too)?

The shoes were to /(too) expensive.

I want (to)/ too run around the planet.

Did you tell her what (to)/ too do first?

This cat is to /(too) chubby.

She handed the parcel (to)/ too the postal worker.

Now see if you can write two sentences, one using **to** and the other using **too**.

Answers may vary

26

In the final activity on this page, you could point out the third spelling: **two**, as in the number. Then, whenever your child says a sentence with **to**, **too** or **two**, you could ask which spelling he or she should use.

Making plurals ★

FACTS

There are certain rules we can follow when making **plurals** of nouns
(see the **Rule** column in the chart below).
However, there are some exceptions to the rules:
Certain nouns change a vowel sound when they become plural.
For example: **tooth/teeth, woman/women** and **mouse/mice.**
Some nouns don't change at all when they become plural.
For example: **deer, sheep** and **species.**

Choose words from the box below and write each one in the correct place on the
chart. Then, write the singular or plural form of the word in the right place, too.

coat	books	buzz	churches	fox	countries
days	key	baby	plays		piano
	loaf		knives	videos	

Rule	Singular	Plural
For most nouns ending in **o**, add **s.**	radio piano video	radios pianos videos
For most nouns ending in **ch, sh, s, x** or **z**, add **es.**	hiss buzz church fox	hisses buzzes churches foxes
For most nouns ending in a vowel and **y**, add **s.**	boy day play key	boys days plays keys
For most nouns ending in a consonant and **y**, drop the **y** and add **ies.**	lily baby country	lilies babies countries
For most nouns ending in a single **f** or **fe**, change the **f** or **fe** to a **v** and add **es.**	half loaf knife	halves loaves knives
For most other nouns, just add **s.**	dog coat book	dogs coats books

Encourage your child to find examples of plural
nouns, such as those on food packaging, shop
signs, adverts and titles of books. Ask your child
to tell you the singular form of these plurals.

★ Similes

FACTS

Similes are phrases that compare one thing to another, using the words
like (for example: Liam roared **like** a lion) or **as** (for example: my grandad
is **as** daft **as** a brush). Poems are a good, fun way of introducing similes.

Look in the word box to find the missing words in this simile poem.
Write them in the spaces below.

| giraffe | welly | busy bee | billy goat | donkey | monkey |

Silly Similes

Here are some silly similes

To make you go, "Tee-hee!"

You're as silly as a ___billy goat___ ,

As manky as a ___monkey___ ,

Smelly like an old ___welly___ ,

Wonky like a three-legged ___donkey___ ,

And as crazy as a lazy ___busy bee___ .

So… if you didn't have a laugh,

Then I'm about as funny as a ___giraffe___ !

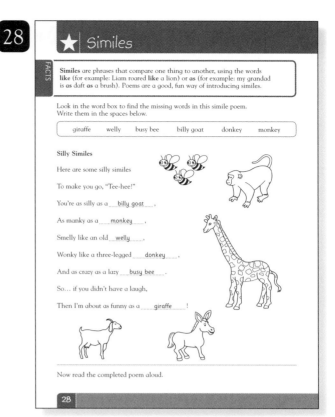

Now read the completed poem aloud.

Invite your child to create some of his or her
own similes. He or she could start with funny
ones about family members!

Writing interesting sentences ★

FACTS

Expanding simple sentences by adding more information helps create a better
picture in the readers' minds. It also makes writing more engaging.

Look at the pictures below and write sentences that describe them.
Use words from the box to make the sentences interesting.

| curly | magic | red | maths | bold | thunder |
| pointy | stripes | excitement | enchanted | strict | grumpy |

Answers may vary

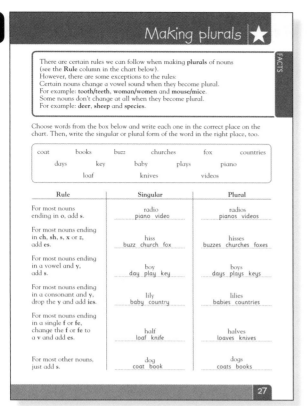

The teacher

The umbrella

The pixie

The woodland

Invite your child to think of some other
interesting sentences from prompts that
you give.

★ Stories and paragraphs

FACTS

A piece of writing, such as a story, is made up of paragraphs. Each paragraph
usually deals with a single theme and is indicated by a new line with
indentation, a small gap between the previous paragraph or, sometimes,
numbering. Paragraphs can range from a single sentence to several sentences.

Whatever type of story you are writing, paragraphs help you structure it. When
you plan a story, plan your paragraphs at the same time. Doing this helps you plot
out the stages of the story, such as the opening, buildup, problem, resolution and
ending. You can use a story mountain plan to help you.

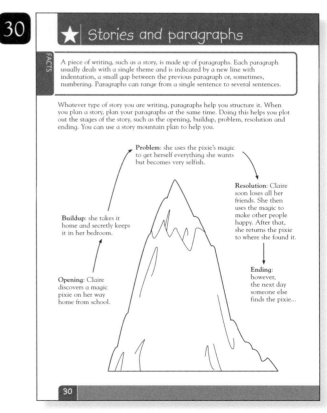

Problem: she uses the pixie's magic
to get herself everything she wants
but becomes very selfish.

Resolution: Claire
soon loses all her
friends. She then
uses the magic to
make other people
happy. After that,
she returns the pixie
to where she found it.

Buildup: she takes it
home and secretly keeps
it in her bedroom.

Ending:
however,
the next day
someone else
finds the pixie...

Opening: Claire
discovers a magic
pixie on her way
home from school.

You might suggest that your child writes
the full story using the example on the story
mountain. Alternatively, he or she might just
tell you the story and you could either write or
type it for him or her.

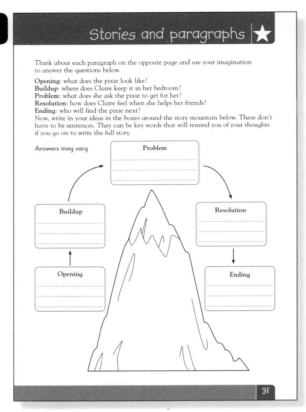

Think about each paragraph on the opposite page and use your imagination to answer the questions below.

Opening: what does the pixie look like?
Buildup: where does Claire keep it in her bedroom?
Problem: what does she ask the pixie to get for her?
Resolution: how does Claire feel when she helps her friends?
Ending: who will find the pixie next?
Now, write in your ideas in the boxes around the story mountain below. These don't have to be sentences. They can be key words that will remind you of your thoughts if you go on to write the full story.

Answers may vary

Problem

Buildup

Resolution

Opening

Ending

Your child may also like to plan a story of his or her own using the story-mountain template.

FACTS Once you have learned the rules associated with spelling, including the use of prefixes and suffixes, it is easier to spell a wider range of words correctly. Another way to learn spelling is the look-cover-write-check method.

Follow the look-cover-write-check method, as shown below, to learn the spelling of the words listed on this page. If you are unsure of the meaning of any of these words, ask your parent to help you look them up in a dictionary.

1. Look (at the word)   2. Cover (the word)

3. Write (the word)   4. Check (to see if you got it right!) ✓

medicine	medicine	address	address
believe	believe	naughty	naughty
woman	woman	various	various
through	through	knowledge	knowledge
experience	experience	quarter	quarter
reign	reign	favourite	favourite
weight	weight	separate	separate
height	height	disappear	disappear
possess	possess	occasion	occasion
island	island	grammar	grammar
library	library	centre	centre

This page will help your child spell these words confidently. Encourage your child to read each word carefully. Test your child on these spellings a day or so later to see how many he or she has remembered.

Glossary

Abstract noun
A word that names a concept or feeling, such as **equality** or **happiness**, that cannot be recognised by our senses, such as sight or hearing.

Adjective
A word that describes a noun. For example, the word **soft** can be used to describe a brush.

Adverb
A word that describes a verb. For example: in the clause **John screamed loudly**, the adverb **loudly** describes the verb **screamed**.

Comma
A punctuation mark that shows where to pause when reading a sentence. It also helps in separating items in a list. For example: **I bought a pencil, an eraser, a ruler and a pen.**

Concrete noun
A word used for naming something that can be recognised by our senses. For example: **muffin**, **lion** or **snow**.

Inverted commas
A punctuation mark (also known as speech marks) used to separate out actual spoken words in a sentence or a longer piece of writing. For example: **John sighed, "We lost the game!"**

Paragraph
A section in a piece of writing that deals with a single theme. It is indicated by indentation, numbering or a small gap.

Plural
A word that refers to more than one of something. We usually, but not always, add an **s** to the singular. For example: **tigers** (tiger), **teeth** (tooth) and **loaves** (loaf).

Preposition
A word that links a noun, pronoun or noun phrase to another word in a sentence.

For example: the monkey was sitting **on** the table.

Pronoun
A word that can take the place of a noun in a sentence. Pronouns include **my**, **he**, **her**, **your**, **their** and **itself**.

Root word
A word without any prefixes or suffixes. For example: **park** is the root word of **parking**, and **tidy** is the root word of **untidy**.

Simile
A phrase that uses **like** or **as** to compare two things. Similes are used to make a piece of writing more interesting. For example: **Edward was as cool as a cucumber before his exam.**

Vowel sound
A long or short speech sound made by the vowels **a**, **e**, **i**, **o**, **u** and sometimes **y**.